NEV~~ER A~~
HAPPIER TIME

Lessons from the War Chapters of Alma
On Achieving Greater Self-Mastery

By J. Reuben Aiton

Certified Life Coach, Eternal Warriors Mentor
and Director of the Eternal Warriors program
for Life Changing Services, LLC

AND

Maurice W. Harker, CMHC

Director of Life Changing Services and
author of *Like Dragons Did They Fight*

This book is a powerful read on its own, but you will find it to be
an excellent companion to the book, *Like Dragons Did They Fight*.

For a Copy of *Like Dragons Did They Fight*, visit:

www.LikeDragonsFree.com

*Dedicated to our wives
and to our team at
Life Changing Services
who provide the inspiration
and driving force for the work
that we accomplish in the fight
for liberty and self-mastery.*

TABLE OF CONTENTS

INTRODUCTION

For many years, we have watched our friends and loved ones experience pain and bondage due to lapses in self-mastery. We, the authors of this book, have also experienced our own pain due to lapses in self-mastery. We have worked very hard to understand not only the psychological science of what happens in the human mind when our behavior crosses the line of our values, but we have carefully and fervently examined the revelations from God to find the eternal principles that will empower us to win the war against Satan who works endlessly to bring us into bondage. It has been miraculous and relieving to find the principles required to succeed right at our fingertips. Please feel our love and dedication to you and your family as you read on...

Throughout the Book of Mormon, several of the book's writers specifically state that they have left their history as an invitation to its readers to come unto Christ. However, Helaman seemed to deviate from this practice when he devoted what became 10% of the entire Book of Mormon to a series of wars fought between the Nephites, Nephite dissenters and Lamanites. Why would Mormon be inspired to outline over 19 chapters of war and intrigue in a book dedicated to inviting its readers to believe in Jesus Christ?

As we carefully examine this series of chapters, we find the reason. These chapters comprise one of the most powerful handbooks on self-mastery and addiction prevention and recovery. They describe not only the wars fought for man's temporal liberty but they metaphorically lay out the spiritual war fought by every man and woman who walks this earth. They describe our enemy, Satan, and his diabolical tactics to bring each of us into bondage.

We come to understand that, contrary to popular world belief, we are not our own worst enemy. Rather, we have an shrewd enemy who wants to destroy God's best and brightest. When you begin to understand this truth, it is incumbent upon you to learn how to "Awaken Your Warrior" and to stand against him with effective battle strategies and defenses.

The Book of Mormon war chapters provide important keys to permanently defeating Satan and living a life of greater self-mastery, happiness and liberty regardless of the calamities unfolding in the world around us. These chapters teach the essence of what it means to enlist and fight with a purpose for our captain, Jesus Christ.

At the May 2016 Air Force Academy Baccalaureate Service, Elder David A. Bednar counseled, "Study the Book of Mormon consistently. Never stop feasting on the words of Christ in all of the scriptures, but especially in the Book of Mormon." He encouraged the cadets to particularly read the Book of Alma. "The chapters describing wars between the Nephites and Lamanites in the Book of Mormon are for you," he said. "It is not merely about temporal tactics but about facing spiritual battles. Learn the intent of the enemy. Study as a disciple of Christ with the focus of coming to battle against Lucifer and his legions."

The important principles taught in the war chapters of Alma go beyond those that are outlined in this book. The principles outlined below are only those that we've gleaned from revelation and our own perspective and experience. However, the Book of Mormon has been beautifully crafted to be an individualized handbook to tell every man "all things what ye should do" (2 Nephi 32:3).

Each of us are encouraged by Nephi to read the words by the power of the Spirit and to "liken them unto ourselves" (1 Nephi 19:23). This book will hopefully inspire its readers to search these chapters with at least one question in mind: What can these words teach me about my own deliverance from captivity to enjoy a life of liberty and self-mastery? For those diligently seeking, there are even more answers to be found than those identified here.

In the following pages, we will outline and expound on the many lessons that we've learned from these powerful chapters. As you read them, we invite you to think about how they apply to your current battles or possible battles you may face as you go through this life.

We hope that as you apply the principles from this book that you will discover like the people of Nephi that, regardless of the wars raging around them, "There never was a happier time among the people of Nephi…" (Alma 50:30). We believe that you can have the same joy during the war that rages on in this mortal existence.

CHAPTER 1

What Is the War in Which We Are Engaged?

A question answered by the war chapters of the Book of Mormon

The war chapters in the Book of Mormon are an important reminder that the war in heaven waged by Lucifer still continues here on the earth. Satan sought to take away the agency of man and to bring all in subjection to himself. Satan promised that he would ensure the salvation of all if God himself would give Satan His glory and power. While this proposal was rejected by two-thirds of the hosts of heaven, Satan and his hosts have never relinquished their desire to take away man's agency and bring them into control and subjection.

Satan knows that if he can influence an individual to forget what he or she values, he can ultimately bring them into bondage. And, so he and his hosts wage a Great War against all of us who chose to keep our first estate and come to this earth clothed in a physical body.

Satan is constantly striving to lead us away from what we value and a remembrance of our reliance upon God. If we forget what we value and what we are fighting to achieve, he can easily lull us into a place of complacency and a loss of purpose. And before we realize it, we find ourselves floating along and blown about by every errant thought or desire. We become disconnected from our Source of Strength and become an easy prey to the desires of the flesh over which Satan has power. His increasing influence can ultimately lead us down a path of addiction, apathy, shrinking from opportunities and a weakening of our ability to consistently keep our word to ourselves or others. In short, when we consistently forget, we become enslaved to Satan's will.

The Book of Mormon outlines story after story of a people who forgot their Source of Strength, protection and power. The period of war that Helaman witnessed was no exception:

> *Thus we see how quick the children of*
> *men do forget the Lord their God, yea,*
> *how quick to do iniquity, and to be led*
> *away by the evil one.*
> – Alma 46:8

The Book of Mormon demonstrates that maintaining our liberty requires an everyday decision to actively hold a spirit of gratitude for our deliverance and to remember our deliverance from bondage.

1 Behold, now it came to pass that the people of Nephi were exceedingly rejoiced, because the Lord had again delivered them out of the hands of their enemies; therefore they gave thanks unto the Lord their God; yea, and they did fast much and pray much, and they did worship God with exceedingly great joy.
– Alma 45:1

28 And it came to pass, that on the other hand, the people of Nephi did thank the Lord their God, because of his matchless power in delivering them from the hands of their enemies.
– Alma 49:28

Captain Moroni warns each of us of the precarious circumstances in which we place ourselves when we forget our deliverance. He censured the government for not providing supplies and resources to fight the long war that had been waged on their behalf.

20 Have ye forgotten the commandments of the Lord your God? Yea, have ye forgotten the captivity of our fathers? Have ye forgotten the many times we have been delivered out of the hands of our enemies?

21 Or do ye suppose that the Lord will still deliver us, while we sit upon our thrones and do not make use of the means which the Lord has provided for us?

22 Yea, will ye sit in idleness while ye are surrounded with thousands of those, yea, and tens of thousands, who do also sit in idleness, while there are thousands round about in the borders of the land who are falling by the sword, yea, wounded and bleeding?

23 Do ye suppose that God will look upon you as guiltless while ye sit still and behold these things? Behold I say unto you, Nay. Now I would that ye should remember that God has said that the inward vessel shall be cleansed first, and then shall the outer vessel be cleansed also.
– Alma 60:20-23

Moroni drives home the importance of not only remembering God's delivering hand but of making use of every resource we have available to firmly defend our kingdom and provide for its protection. He warns those who become complacent from what appears to be a safe and protected place. And, he challenges us all to become more watchful and vigilant in remembering why we are safe and take daily action to maintain that safety.

We have worked with many individuals who, after breaking free of debilitating patterns and addictions, have eventually found themselves once again trapped in Satan's web. These individuals' stories are almost always the same. They forgot the basics that connected them to God's strength and that originally led to their deliverance.

When we enjoy periods of peace, one of Satan's greatest tactics is to lull us into a sense of carnal security and distract us from the basics. It's important to remember the question that is answered by almost the entire Book of Mormon: "When will the Lamanites stop attacking the Nephites?" The answer: "When all of the Nephites are dead." Satan and his forces will never stop the attempt to destroy us and all that we love. So we must always remember our deliverance.

Following many years of war, Helaman describes the success that the Nephites experienced both spiritually and temporally when they learned the important lessons of remembering and of humility.

> *48 And the people of Nephi began to prosper again in the land, and began to multiply and to wax exceedingly strong again in the land. And they began to grow exceedingly rich.*
>
> *49 But notwithstanding their riches, or their strength, or their prosperity, they were not*

*lifted up in the pride of their eyes; neither were
they slow to remember the Lord their God; but
they did humble themselves exceedingly before
him.*

*50 Yea, they did remember how great things
the Lord had done for them, that he had
delivered them from death, and from bonds,
and from prisons, and from all manner of
afflictions, and he had delivered them out of
the hands of their enemies.*

*51 And they did pray unto the Lord their God
continually, insomuch that the Lord did bless
them, according to his word, so that they did
wax strong and prosper in the land.*
– Alma 62:48-51

As individuals have embraced the strategies of "remembering" that we teach in both our recovery and prevention programs, they have found a connection to strength and power that enables them to consistently win their battles. Our most successful clients will cite the fact that they have now gone for years without missing a single day of doing their MAN or GRL PWR goals and have also gone for years without a lost battle to their addictions or debilitating habits.

The connection is clear. When we find ways to remember our deliverance and consistently stay connected to our Source of Strength, we will win all of our battles.

Satan's Biochemical Warfare

Satan has learned a powerful biochemical recipe for quickly lulling the human brain's "values/creativity" center to sleep and leaving us in a state of forgetfulness. We call his method the Satanic Spin™. The details of the Satanic Spin™ are explained in Maurice's companion book *Like Dragons Did They Fight.* Visit *LikeDragonsFree.com* to obtain a free electronic copy of this book and learn more about Satan's biochemical tactics.

When individuals understand Satan's biochemical spin, they can become more aware of the specific ways that he disconnects them from remembering. This new awareness is powerful and enables each individual to activate an effective antidote known as Warrior Chemistry™.

Warrior Chemistry™ reactivates our ability to remember. Captain Moroni understood this antidote when he raised the Title of Liberty and moved an entire nation into righteous action. The Sons of Helaman understood it each time that they chose to hold fast against impossible odds. All of the great warriors of the Book of Mormon who exercised righteous ferocity experienced the liberating power of Warrior Chemistry™.

From modern neuroscience, we understand that intentional righteous ferocity can activate chemicals within our brain that stimulate the frontal lobe. The frontal lobe is vital in that it is the center of our values and creativity. This center has previously been lulled to sleep as a result of the Satanic Spin™ and needs to be awakened if we are to remember what we value and to see ways to connect those values to specific creative actions.

When Captain Moroni raised the Title of Liberty, he was helping the Nephites to remember what they were fighting to protect. The words of the Title were simple and reminded every warrior of their deepest love and commitment:

> *"In memory of our God, our religion, and freedom, and our peace, our wives, and our children."*
> *– Alma 46:12*

By remembering what we are fighting for and why we are fighting, we can activate Warrior Chemistry™ just as Captain Moroni did for his people. This remembrance strengthens our resolve to draw a clear line in the sand with the enemy and to take back our power.

Key Takeway From This Chapter

We fight a War of Remembering. Remembering our constant reliance upon God and our most treasured values awakens the Warrior within each of us and connects us with all of the power needed to win our battles. Every warrior who is awakened feels a natural craving to fight for the cause of freedom for himself and for those whom he loves.

CHAPTER 2

What Is the Cause for Which You Fight?

We are constantly at war spiritually and sometimes even physically. If we are to win our most important battles, we must have a sufficient, motivating cause to fight daily. Does our cause motivate us sufficiently to stand our ground despite the strength and progress of our foe? Would we be willing to give our lives for that cause?

Consider the motivation of wicked Amalackiah who sought to bring the Nephite nation into bondage versus the motivation of the righteous Nephites who sought only for liberty:

> *8 For behold, his (Amalackiah's) designs were to stir up the Lamanites to anger against the Nephites; this he did that he might usurp great power over them, and also that he might gain power over the Nephites by bringing them into bondage.*

9 And now the design of the Nephites was to support their lands, and their houses, and their wives, and their children, that they might preserve them from the hands of their enemies; and also that they might preserve their rights and their privileges, yea, and also their liberty, that they might worship God according to their desires.
– Alma 43:8-9

Notice that both Amalackiah and the Nephites had a clear purpose behind their actions. If we are to win our battles, we need more than just purpose. We need a clear, *righteous* purpose.

Without a clear, righteous cause, it can become extremely challenging to hold our ground when the enemy is unleashing his fury upon us. A righteous cause connects our hearts with God and unlocks the powers of heaven to come to our aid.

One form of bondage is "addiction". Having a "bad habit" can be difficult to break and can be thought of as a form of bondage as well. If you are not sure whether the modern day "Lamanites" or demons, have been attacking you, check to see if you have any bad habits that you are struggling to overpower. If you do, then it is time to consider that you are battling intelligent spiritual opponents. A primary purpose of this book is to help you recognize your enemy and to escape any form of bondage.

When we have a righteous cause, it can turn the tide of seemingly impossible situations to our favor. Consider how the righteous desires of the Nephites motivated them to win despite what appeared to be imminent defeat:

> *45 Nevertheless, the Nephites were inspired by a better cause, for they were not fighting for monarchy nor power but they were fighting for their homes and their liberties, their wives and their children, and their all, yea, for their rites of worship and their church.*

> *46 And they were doing that which they felt was the duty which they owed to their God; for the Lord had said unto them, and also unto their fathers, that: Inasmuch as ye are not guilty of the first offense, neither the second, ye shall not suffer yourselves to be slain by the hands of your enemies.*

> *47 And again, the Lord has said that: Ye shall defend your families even unto bloodshed. Therefore for this cause were the Nephites contending with the Lamanites, to defend themselves, and their families, and their lands, their country, and their rights, and their religion.*

*48 And it came to pass that when the men of
Moroni saw the fierceness and the anger of
the Lamanites, they were about to shrink and
flee from them. And Moroni, perceiving their
intent, sent forth and inspired their hearts
with these thoughts—yea, the thoughts of their
lands, their liberty, yea, their freedom from
bondage.*
– Alma 43:45-47

We have found that those who come to us for help and are about to lose opportunities to serve missions or their spouse and family as a result of addiction have developed a keen motivation to fight. The cost of defeat has become perilously high.

We have also observed that our addiction recovery programs are filled by the hundreds every year. In contrast, relatively few individuals trickle into our prevention program, which teaches the same tools and principles as the recovery programs. Can we find a motivation to fight before the stakes are so high?

Someone once said that God first uses a feather (still, small voice), then a hammer and then a Mack truck to get our attention. We can begin to notice God's "feathers" early on and develop the strength to withstand the attacks of the adversary before losing so much ground and leaving so many casualties in the wake of our decisions.

Moroni inspired freedom with a cause that motivated an entire nation when he crafted the Title of Liberty:

> *12 And it came to pass that he rent his coat; and he took a piece thereof, and wrote upon it—In memory of our God, our religion, and freedom, and our peace, our wives, and our children— and he fastened it upon the end of a pole.*

> *13 And he fastened on his head-plate, and his breastplate, and his shields, and girded on his armor about his loins; and he took the pole, which had on the end thereof his rent coat, (and he called it the title of liberty) and he bowed himself to the earth, and he prayed mightily unto his God for the blessings of liberty to rest upon his brethren, so long as there should a band of Christians remain to possess the land.*
> *– Alma 46:12-13*

Some of the greatest national leaders in our world's history created similar rally cries that moved entire nations into action...men like Abraham Lincoln, George Washington and Winston Churchill. Others, like Joseph Smith, Brigham Young, Martin Luther King and Gandhi, inspired entire movements with a clear vision that they held for a better life and a better world.

We challenge you to find a purpose that motivates you in the same way that the people of Ammon were motivated. They were so committed to their purpose and covenant that they would not abandon it even if it meant losing their lives.

> *Yea, and they also knew the extreme hatred of the Lamanites towards their brethren, who were the people of Anti-Nephi-Lehi, who were called the people of Ammon—**and they would not take up arms, yea, they had entered into a covenant and they would not break it— therefore, if they should fall into the hands of the Lamanites they would be destroyed.***
> *– Alma 46:12-13; Alma 43:11*

Many who enlist in the cause of freedom, whether it be due to depression, anxiety, poor habits or addiction, still find themselves falling down over and over again. Some of their casualties are spouses, family members or close associates. This can feel challenging for everyone.

Long-term success requires that we bury all of the destructive weapons that are hurting us and our loved ones while arming ourselves with protective weapons. Burying destructive weapons may come at the cost of our own comfort. It may require us to sacrifice our point of view. It may necessitate burying all of our ego and self-satisfying behaviors in order to give our complete care and devotion to another. When our purpose is clear and we allow ourselves to be transformed by our love for it, we can exercise the same resilience as the people of Ammon.

Even though we must be willing to lay down all of our destructive weapons, consider also the following verse as you ponder to what degree we must be ready to hold fast to our God-given purpose:

> *Now the descendents were as numerous,*
> *nearly, as were the Nephites; and thus the*
> *Nephites were obliged to contend with their*
> *brethren, even unto bloodshed.*
> *– Alma 43:14*

Let us not forget how intensely we will need to prepare and to fight our adversary in order to win. So many of the warriors I work with look at me with some confusion as I train them. They ask with their words or with their eyes, "Why are you pushing us so hard? Why do you take this battle so seriously? Why can't you back off a little bit?" This includes marriages that have been brutalized to the point of death or near death. If we don't fight hard, and if we don't train hard, marriages and families will be destroyed.

A Powerful Protective Weapon: A Definite Purpose

A popular idea for many years now has been to run away from temptation. While this may have been adequate in the past, the Book of Mormon tells us that when an enemy threatens to destroy us and/or put us in bondage, we need to be prepared with weapons of war as well as shields to defend.

> *And it came to pass that he met the Lamanites in the borders of Jershon, and his people were* <u>*armed*</u> *with* **swords**, *and with* **cimeters**, *and with* **all manner of weapons of war**.

> *And when the armies of the Lamanites saw that the people of Nephi, or that Moroni, had prepared his people with* **breastplates** *and with* **arm-shields**, *yeah and also* **shields to defend their heads**, *and also they were dressed with* **thick clothing...**
> *– Alma 43:18-19*

In this book, and in *Like Dragons Did They Fight*, you will see that we have found powerful methods and weapons with which to fight and that these methods have been available since the time that the Book of Mormon was given to us. One of the most powerful weapons available to each of us is to have a **Definite Purpose** for our life.

Moroni and the Sons of Helaman both exemplified lives of deep purpose. It was this purpose that protected them from both physical danger and Satan's power. Consider again the description of Moroni:

> *11 And Moroni was a strong and a mighty man; he was a man of a perfect understanding; yea, a man that did not delight in bloodshed; a man whose soul did joy in the liberty and the freedom of his country, and his brethren from bondage and slavery;*

> *12 Yea, a man whose heart did swell with thanksgiving to his God, for the many privileges and blessings which he bestowed upon his people; a man who did labor exceedingly for the welfare and safety of his people.*

> *13 Yea, and he was a man who was firm in the faith of Christ, and he had sworn with an oath to defend his people, his rights, and his country, and his religion, even to the loss of his blood.*

> *17 Yea, verily, verily I say unto you, if all men had been, and were, and ever would be, like*

*unto Moroni, behold, the very powers of hell
would have been shaken forever; yea, the devil
would never have power over the hearts of the
children of men.*

*18 Behold, he was a man like unto Ammon,
the son of Mosiah, yea, and even the other sons
of Mosiah, yea, and also Alma and his sons,
for they were all men of God.*
– Alma 48:11-13, 17-18

Moroni demonstrated that when we hold fast to a definite purpose, Satan can have no power over us. It is only when we drift from that purpose or choose to float along through life with no purpose at all that Satan begins to gain ground over our lives.

To win this war, you will need to become "like unto" Moroni. It may sound intimidating, but it need not be. If you were to ask Moroni how to become amazing like him, he most likely would describe a process similar to what President Nelson has been teaching: "Line upon line, grace for grace, just like Christ grew up as well."

Do not be overwhelmed. You can do it. Keep learning from Moroni's example and, line upon line, you will hold fast in your definite purpose.

There is a major difference between being "busy" and being "on purpose." If we aren't watchful, we can find our lives completely filled with busyness and distractions that actually prevent us from living our purpose.

Knowing where to focus our energy might feel challenging. Life is typically filled with a laundry list of tasks and demands that press upon us. Not all of them are critical to our success. Satan often uses shame to keep us in a place of feeling overwhelmed with all of the things that we "should" be doing.

Notice the energy of "should" versus the energy of "could." When we shift our daily question from *"What should I be doing today?"* to *"What could I do today that would enable me to focus on my most important purpose here on earth?"* we can feel an entirely different connection to possibility. We can more fully connect to the Spirit of God and be open to His whisperings.

When we connect to the Spirit, we will feel guided to the activities that enable us to fully partner with God. As a partner, we will find that we don't have to be able to "do it all." We can offer our full gift and trust that God will accept it and multiply it.

There is an important key to knowing when the Spirit is guiding you in a certain direction of focus. Notice what you feel **interested** in pursuing. **Our interests can be God's breadcrumbs leading us to our purpose.**

That being said, not all of our interests are God-given. A God-given interest always meets three criteria:

1. It edifies,

2. It expands the mind and

3. It enlarges the Spirit. A God-given interest will usually lead us to activities centered around saving others' lives.

Maintaining a definite purpose requires three key elements: **Decision, Focus** and **Belief.** We must clearly **Decide** what we want and make a choice to hold fast to that decision regardless of the price. We **Focus** our energy and efforts on our purpose, pushing aside anything that would distract us from it. And, we continue stepping forward while utilizing all of our resources to achieve that purpose and holding a firm **Belief** in the power of God to help us succeed. We hold fast even when failure or death might seem imminent.

Consider the Sons of Helaman, who were miraculously protected time and time again from physical danger and death by the purpose which they firmly maintained:

> *16 But behold, it came to pass they had many sons, who had not entered into a covenant that they would not take their weapons of war to defend themselves against their enemies; therefore they did assemble themselves together*

at this time, as many as were able to take up
arms, and they called themselves Nephites.

17 And they entered into a covenant to fight
for the liberty of the Nephites, yea, to protect
the land unto the laying down of their lives;
yea, even they covenanted that they never
would give up their liberty, but they would
fight in all cases to protect the Nephites and
themselves from bondage.
– Alma 53:16-17

The Sons of Helaman held a purpose that was completely clear and definite. There was no turning back for them even if it meant death. Each of these young men chose to stay laser-focused on that purpose. And, they demonstrated an unwavering faith in God in every action they took.

Taking Upon a Name – Identity Anchoring

Finding a definite purpose for our lives requires a very key shift from reaction-based behavior to proactive living. Reaction-based behavior describes situations where you come to the conclusion that you did what you did because of what someone or something else did to you first. Examples include:

- "I was passive aggressive, because my wife didn't meet my needs."

- "I was mean to him, because he didn't talk to me."

- "I didn't finish my homework, because I don't like the teacher."

- "I am not going to become religious, because my parents would say 'told you so'".

- "I did not fight against the Lamanites because that would take up too much time and money."

In contrast, proactive-based thinking requires that we take responsibility for our actions and choose how we will act based on the values that we hold.

There is a powerful way to become proactive. It's called "Identity Anchoring." Alma 46:15 demonstrates a form of Identity Anchoring:

> *15 And those who did belong to the church were faithful; yea, all those who were true believers in Christ took upon them, gladly, the name of Christ, or Christians as they were called, because of their belief in Christ who should come.*
> *– Alma 46:15*

Notice that the Nephites choose to anchor their identity with Jesus Christ. They remained faithful to that identity regardless of how others acted towards them.

We have human brains. And, we have an enemy who likes to sabotage us. We must be intentional, not reactional, about what we do and how we respond to what goes on around us. There are three key ways that we can be intentional:

1. Discern that you are under attack.

2. Initiate a pre-planned, pre-trained response.

3. Dominate, don't just survive.

A big surprise that I've discovered as a therapist is the need for my clients to add psychological training to the "insight" part of the therapeutic experience. When I went through graduate school, "insight" or "ah-ha moments" or "paradigm shifting" was the central goal of the therapeutic experience. It is true that it is very difficult to make desired progress in therapy without insight, but it is also insufficient. The brain needs a pathway, a series of highspeed, pre-planned, pre-practiced responses in order to execute preferred behaviors.

The brain is capable, with practice to be very high speed and accurate. Think of musicians as an example. With practice, they can execute many highspeed, accurate movements of their ten fingers. (For more on this, read https://www.

lifechangingservices.org/2011/11/10/musicians-athletes-soldiers-and/)

To dominate, be sure that in your practice/training sessions, you always end with something small, medium or large that brings good into the life of someone else. In other words, do something that makes someone else's life better.

Keep a list of these types of things in your pocket so you don't have to think of something in the moment. A primary reason for Satanic attacks is to distract us from using our gifts and talents to serve those around us. When in doubt, start by doing good for your mom or your wife. As Captain Moroni might have said to the Lamanites after attacking the Nephites, you want to be able to say, "You should not have messed with me (and my team of Warriors)!"

You can become proactive and live with a definite purpose by choosing to anchor your identity to that of a warrior. Regularly return to that identity everyday. Pre-plan and practice your response with examples like these:

- "When my wife did not meet my needs, I made sure the family had dinner and cleaned up afterward."

- "When _____ didn't talk to me, I made a special effort to express kindness and gratitude to them."

- "I found myself not liking my teacher, so I took the time to get to know them better and found out they are stressed out about a child they have at home that has cancer."

- "I was worried my parents would say 'I told you so', so because I decided to be a humble person, I went to them and thanked them for teaching me as a child so I knew what to turn to as I grew older."

- "I decided I am a man who will do what it takes to protect my family, so I decided to take the time and invest the money needed to learn how to be a great modern-day warrior."

Connecting Regularly to Our Definite Purpose

Throughout history, military leaders have needed to help their men elevate themselves from their day-to-day psychological functioning processes to a higher level needed to prepare for and engage in war. Modern psychologists now consider this influencing method a key part of Motivational Interviewing. This repetitious listing of "reasons for fighting" can be done as an individual, but is usually most effective when done as a team.

If you are a warrior who is striving to align your behaviors in closer harmony with God, start by clarifying your primary battle right now. Describe what consists of a "win" to you, and on the flip side of the same coin, what you would consider a "lost battle."

Now, list a half dozen reasons why you are fighting to win this battle. Create a system to review these reasons three or more times per day while making an effort to elevate your emotional investment each time.

Key Takeaway From This Chapter

As you consider the causes that motivate you to action, we challenge you to find one that deeply stirs your heart, that connects you to God's power and that impacts the world in a positive way even if only one person at a time. A righteous, definite purpose has the power to protect, to enliven and to deliver us from our most challenging foes.

CHAPTER 3

Understanding Our Enemy

If we are to defeat our enemy, we must first understand him and his diabolical strategies. One of Satan's favorite tactics is to hide in the shadows and be completely transparent. From his hidden places of attack, he can easily defeat us again and again. He laughs as we reel in anguish with a belief that we are our own worst enemy and that we are fundamentally broken in some way. He doesn't want us to realize that he and his demons are the ones attacking us.

If Satan is attacking you often, it's not because you're broken. It's because you are one of the great and noble leaders whom he wants to disable and destroy before you become a threat to his purposes.

Consider the following verse as you ponder what is required to be ready for an attack from an enemy like Satan.

> *For behold, it came to pass that the Zoramites became Lamanites; therefore, in the commencement of the eighteenth year the people of the Nephites saw that the Lamanites*

were coming upon them; therefore, they made
preparations for war; yea, they gathered
together their armies in the land of Jershon.
– Alma 43:4

This verse reminds us of three of the early stages of war. We must "see" that the enemy is real, that he is a real threat, and that he is coming. We must make preparations. We cannot just "wing it" and hope to successfully win our battles. And it is so very wise to gather together with fellow warriors who are preparing for battle. *[If you have not already done so, perhaps now is the time to join up with a team of Eternal Warriors!* **Visit EternalWarriorsTraining.org** *to learn more.]*

As we begin to understand our enemy and prepare to meet him, consider the following verse:

And he [Captain Moroni] also knowing that it
was the only desire of the Nephites to preserve
their lands and their liberty, and their church,
therefore he thought it no sin that he should
*defend them by **stratagem**; therefore, he found*
by his spies** which course the Lamanites **were
***to take**.*
– Alma 43:30

There are two important principles found in this verse. This is the first verse in the Book of Mormon where the word "stratagem" appears. It is only found in six other verses, all of which are located in the next 15 chapters of Alma. Captain Moroni brings to our attention that now is the time for more sophisticated preparation against a very intelligent and determined enemy.

Quite often, when it comes to self-mastery issues, the primary strategy today has been to overcome it with strength, submission or willpower. However, the Book of Mormon, which was written for our day, indicates a more effective tactic. The battlefield with Satan is primarily a psychological battlefield where stratagem is required.

Captain Moroni was always aware and seriously conscientious about the intelligence and cruelty of his enemy. Most of the people of the Nephites had responsibilities that revolved around caring for things at home. A rare few, like Captain Moroni, were given the responsibility, as spies, to observe and study the enemy for the sake of the people's safety. This is our job as therapists and coaches. A handful of very carefully trained psychological warriors have been spying on Satan and his demons for over 25 years. We have been carefully breaking down the elements of psychological, emotional, cognitive and psycho-biochemical attacks on you and your loved ones (the details of our findings and what to do about it can be found in this book and the book, *Like Dragons Did They Fight*. Get the Free eBook at **LikeDragonsFree.org**)

We hope you have no need for us. We hope you can peacefully enjoy your homes, families and communities. But if not....

we are ready to train you. We are ready to teach you the most cutting edge Satanic attacks like "The Radio Trick", "Neurological Biochemical Warfare", and "Psychological Civil War" for starters.

We are ready to teach you how to discern and detect the most subtle of Satanic attacks. We will train you to respond as any Warrior would respond with speed, accuracy and strength. Like the Warriors of the Book of Mormon, you will align yourself with God and your fellow warriors. You don't need to figure it out all on your own. We "spies" have been studying "which course the "demons" will take for a very long time. You are in good hands.

Characteristics of the Enemy

What are the characteristics of our enemy? How does he fight? Consider some of the following verses which provide a clearer view of him:

> *29 And now, as Moroni knew the intention*
> *of the Lamanites [**or demons**], that it was*
> *their intention to **destroy** their brethren, or **to***
> ***subject them** and **bring them into bondage***
> *that **they might establish a kingdom** unto*
> *themselves over the land;*
> *– Alma 43:29*

We are reminded again how important it is to keep in

mind the mentality of our enemies...They are really serious about destroying and bringing us and our loved ones into bondage. Satan is looking for any way possible to bring us into subjection and bondage whether it be physical, spiritual, financial, mental or emotional in nature. It doesn't matter to him as long as he can establish his "kingdom" on earth and amass as many willing or unwilling followers as he can.

Men are that they might have joy. The wars we fight in this lifetime don't have to drag us down, consume us or leave us reeling in fear. But, to be happy and secure in this lone and dreary world, you need to prepare for the true nature of your opponent.

So, just how "bad" or "mean" is our enemy? Consider a tactic used by Zerahemnah when he went against the Nephites:

> 6 And now, as the Amalekites **were of a more wicked and murderous disposition** that the Lamanites were, in and of themselves, therefore Zerahemnah appointed chief captains over the Lamanites, and they were all Amalekites and Zoramites.
>
> 7 Now this he did **that he might preserve their hatred towards the Nephites,** that he might bring them into subjection to the accomplishment of his designs.
> – Alma 43: 6-7

It is important that we remember the personality of our opponent. Most of us accidentally think, "He really can't be that bad or that mean." Unfortunately, underestimating our enemy is one of the fastest ways to lose a battle. In the same way that you, my good warrior, were saved for the last days to bring your glorious gifts and strong spirit to give good and fight evil, the dark one saved his "most wicked, murderous and hate filled" demons and strategies for the last days.

Notice from this next verse that, just like the Lamanites, Satan is vigilantly watching for specific places to attack:

> *And it came to pass that the word of the Lord came unto Alma, and Alma informed the messengers of Moroni, that the armies of the Lamanites were marching round about in the wilderness, that they might come over into the land of Manti, **that they might commence an attack upon the weaker part of the people**.*
> *– Alma 43:24*

This verse reminds us that Satan's demons are dirty fighters. They always go for the weakest spots of those who are his greatest enemies. It is critically important that we recognize that we have weaknesses and that we can't win our battles if we refuse to be aware of them.

Ether 12:27 provides the solution to how we can become aware of our weaknesses and shift them from weak places to "strongholds:"

27 And if men come unto me [Jesus Christ speaking] I will show unto them their weakness. I give unto men weakness that they may be humble; and my grace is sufficient for all men that humble themselves before me; for if they humble themselves before me, and have faith in me, then will I make weak things become strong unto them.
– Ether 12:27

God knew that, if we didn't stay open and connected to Him, we wouldn't be able to succeed. So, He provides the unexpected blessing of weakness as a way to help us stay open and in a state of listening and obedience. And, as long as we stay aligned with Jesus Christ, His promise is that whatever weakness we are experiencing will be made strong. Satan will not prevail against that "weaker place" just as the Lamanites didn't prevail against the weaker places of the Nephites when Captain Moroni sent sufficient strength to defend them.

The first part of Alma 43:24, And it came to pass that the word of the Lord came unto Alma…, gives us confidence that if keep Prophets involved (study scriptures and conference talks), we will be more able to know where the enemy is going to attack. This is one aspect of coming unto Jesus. Look for your weak spots through the Prophets' counsels. Where and when have you lost battles before? What mood are you in when the enemy starts to talk you into considering behaviors that contradict your values system? Use prophetic counsel as a guide to know where and when the enemy will attack your weak places and how to have them sufficiently fortified.

We may experience times in our lives when it looks like the demons (in the form of temptations and torments) withdraw for a time. And, many times they intentionally do withdraw to lull us into a sense of false security. When this happens, it is easy to feel like just taking a break. The following verse reinforces that when you have a serious enemy, you need Spies and Prophets to really stay a step ahead of your enemy.

> But it came to pass, as soon as they had
> departed into the wilderness **Moroni sent spies**
> **into the wilderness to watch their camp**; and
> Moroni, also **knowing of the prophecies of**
> **Alma, sent certain men unto him**, desiring
> him that he should inquire of the Lord whither
> the armies of the Nephites should go to defend
> themselves against the Lamanites.
> – Alma 43:23

In our experience working with warriors of all ages, you can be trained to be a spy and acquire the gift of prophecy for yourself and your stewardship.

Try these two steps:

1. Pray (connect with God) for God to help you see what's coming.

2. Guess how the enemy could attack. Guessing is a form of thinking. Thinking while plugged into God is a form of pondering. Pondering about the future is the beginning of Prophesying.

We are aware that you may not have tried very hard to think and plan like a mean and destructive person. But, if you are going to stay a step ahead of your enemy, just ask this question after completing Step (1) above: "What are the demons going to try next?" (A careful and detailed walkthrough of this process is found in the discussion under Question 6 of the Captain's Log in *Like Dragons Did They Fight*. Visit **LikeDragonsFree.com**). As we use this process, we can learn to be "as wise as serpents and as harmless as doves." (Matthew 10:16)

When I first meet a new warrior, I will commonly ask them when and where they are guessing the enemy will attack next. Often I will get a blank face response or they will say, "Any time, any where." This is a Satanic trick designed to cause constant panic and psychological exhaustion. In reality, on most days, there are only one to three significant Satanic attacks, and they are usually very predictable based on past patterns. When you work with a Warrior Trainer, you can learn to identify these patterns in advance and prepare for them. Instead of being in a state of fear, you will feel confident and powerful, always a step ahead of your enemy. You will be prepared to meet him, always "crushing his head" before he has a chance to get any momentum.

It's important to remember one other key characteristic of Satan's demons that is demonstrated in the following verse:

> *But they were not armed with breastplates, nor shields—therefore, **they were exceedingly afraid of the armies of the Nephites because of their armor**, notwithstanding their number being so much greater than the Nephites.*
> *– Alma 43:21*

While the idea of demons can be very scary, let this verse remind us that even though there are probably more demons than there are mortals, they really are scared of us. When we have adequate protection systems including a definite purpose, when we have better weapons, and when we are aligned with God and His ministering angels, we will find that "Those that be with us are more than those that be with them" – 2 Kings 6:16.

Two Prevalent Satanic Attack Tactics: Flattery and Forgetfulness

There are a wide variety of tactics that the enemy regularly employs to bring us into bondage and subjection to him. However, In the first eight verses of Alma 46, Captain Moroni observes that the happiness and stability of his people are threatened by two major psychological attacks: flatteries and forgetfulness.

Check yourself – Are you being tricked by modern-day, subtle, Satanic flatteries? Flatteries refer to stimulations of your feelings sufficient to influence you to behave contrary to your values system. When you are deciding what to do with your mental, emotional and physical time, are you consulting the "feel like it", or mood part of your brain or are you consulting the values part of your brain regarding which course of action to take?

If you look at the pattern, the stronger the *Flattery*, the more *Forgetful* we become of our true Values Systems. When people have Lost Battles (behaviors contrary to their values systems), if asked why they lost that battle, they almost universally reply, "I forgot," referring to what was important to them.

Unfortunately, in our English language we do not have separate words in our vocabulary for words like "want" and "desire" to distinguish between mood-based wants and values-based wants. For instance, "I want to be lazy" (mood-based) and "I want to go exercise" (values-based) both use the same feeling verb. This may seem like a little thing, but it is causing substantial difficulties in individual and relationship psychology. When asked, "What do you want?" a great deal of confusion can ensue. Even, "What do you really want?" doesn't separate mood from values.

I can think of at least one husband who flip flops between mood-based wants and values-based wants over and over. His wife feels like she is in a tug of war between two men: one who wants to be married to her and one who doesn't.

Alma 46:32 declares that Captain Moroni, "did according to his desires". These were not mood-based desires. In describing Moroni's actions in this verse, we observe that he was focused on observing the needs of his people and going to great lengths to inspire them to take action and lead them into battle.

Flatteries can be defined as anything that pulls us away from what we value due to a mood. Look for decisions you make or actions you take based on "I don't feel like it," or "I feel like it." When I work with a client and ask them something like, "How did you decide whether or not to do your reading at that time?" if they say anything like "I felt like it" or "I didn't feel like it," I know that I am dealing with a troublesome situation.

On a spiritual level, if we regularly make decisions based on moods, we are accidentally, but legitimately breaking the 2nd commandment that Moses brought down from the mountain: "Thou shalt have no other Gods before me." Accidentally, subtly ("the serpent was the most subtle of all the beasts of the field"), our moods have become our god if we are using them to make decisions. That which leads us, that which we follow, becomes our god.

Check yourself...look over the last 24-48 hours, how many times did you think about something or take action on something based on your values in comparison to based on your "feel like it's?"

On a psychological science level, I can tell a lot about a client's addiction susceptibility level based on the frequency of mood-based decisions and the ratio of mood-based to values-based decisions. The more mood-based their decisions are, the more at risk they are to staying in or falling into an addiction. The more values-based their decisions are, the less likely they are to fall into addiction.

We challenge you. For the next 24 hours, pay very close attention to the high-speed questions in your brain that are intended to help you decide how to spend your mental, emotional and physical time. Especially watch for questions like, "What do I want to do today?" Or, "What do I feel like doing today/ right now?" Compare that to, "What would be important for me to do today?" Or, "What would be wise for me to do today/ right now?" We challenge you to firmly resolve that all of your decisions for one day will be values-based instead of mood-based. To succeed in this, you will probably have to set up an effective reminder system like those taught in our prevention and recovery programs.

Key Takeaway From This Chapter

If we are to defeat our enemy, we must go beyond mere strength and fortitude. We need to develop effective stratagem against a psychological genius who has been perfecting his battle techniques for over 6000 years. We can not underestimate his hatred for us and his constant persistence in looking for our weaknesses. We must always stay aligned with the Savior so that our weaknesses can become our strengths. And, we must never forget that, when we are properly armed with the right strategies, the enemy will retreat in fear though their numbers may be greater than ours.

CHAPTER 4

Qualities of Successful Warriors

If our desire is to defeat Satan, we can learn the types of characteristics that would make us powerful and successful warriors when we study men like Moroni, Pahoran and the sons of Helaman. These men consistently succeeded in protecting themselves and their nation.

What were some of these warriors most important qualities? From the following verses, we glean a few.

Moroni

> *11 And Moroni was a strong and a mighty man; he was a man of a perfect understanding; yea, a man that did not delight in bloodshed; a man whose soul did joy in the liberty and the freedom of his country, and his brethren from bondage and slavery;*
>
> *12 Yea, a man whose heart did swell with thanksgiving to his God, for the many privileges and blessings which he bestowed*

upon his people; a man who did labor exceedingly for the welfare and safety of his people.

13 Yea, and he was a man who was firm in the faith of Christ, and he had sworn with an oath to defend his people, his rights, and his country, and his religion, even to the loss of his blood.
– Alma 48:11-13

"A strong and mighty man..." Consider for a few moments what actions you could take to build strength and mightiness in your life. With an understanding of how brain chemistry affects self-mastery, we can go into the gym of the mind and build mental strength and mightiness by exercising the 'values' center of our brain over the 'preference' center of our brain.

Every time we make a choice to act from our values, we fire the "values" center of the brain and wire neural pathways that make it easier to make subsequent decisions for self-mastery. This builds mental and spiritual strength and can make us mighty over time.

"A man of perfect understanding..." Consider how you could increase your understanding through your personal daily studies and by implementing the light and knowledge you receive from direct revelation.

"A man whose soul did joy in the liberty and freedom of his country..." Do you have an all-encompassing purpose for your life? What is your cause of freedom and liberty? Are you willing to fully adopt it and fight for it until it is achieved?

"A man whose heart did swell with thanksgiving to his God..." Moroni understood that feeling gratitude for our blessings and holding gratitude in any of our circumstances unlocks a power of abundance that enables us to transcend any bondage.

"A man who did labor exceedingly for the welfare and safety of his people..." Over whom have you been given stewardship? How exceedingly are you laboring for their welfare over your own?

"He was a man who was firm in the faith of Christ..." Moroni knew his Source of Strength and continually sought to align himself with the Savior and to exercise his faith daily with the resources placed under his stewardship.

"He had sworn with an oath to defend...even to the loss of his blood..." Moroni's cause went deeper than his own life. His commitment to his goal had no limits.

We also learn several important qualities that Captain Moroni possessed from the following verse:

And it came to pass that they did stop and withdrew a pace from them. And Moroni said unto Zerahemnah: Behold, Zerahemnah, that we do not desire to be men of blood. Ye know that ye are in our hands, yet we do not desire to slay you.
– Alma 44:1

Captain Moroni understood that his strength, intensity and ferocious dedication were powers given from God like unto fire. Like any other strong emotion produced from body chemistry, these powers were never intended to take over, control the body and mind, and govern thoughts and actions.

Captain Moroni had the necessary self-awareness to tone it down when necessary. He could stop and withdraw as needed. He recognized his values, and his values were stronger than his intensity.

Whenever we fight for something we must always remember why we are fighting. Warrior Chemistry is a gift from God to empower us to protect our loved ones as needed. It is not for the purpose of blind, uncontrolled destruction.

The Sons of Helaman

Consider the qualities exhibited by the sons of Helaman in the following verses:

20 And they were all young men, and they were exceedingly valiant for courage, and also for strength and activity; but behold, this was not all—they were men who were true at all times in whatsoever thing they were entrusted.

21 Yea, they were men of truth and soberness, for they had been taught to keep the commandments of God and to walk uprightly before him.
– Alma 53:20-21

"...they were exceedingly valiant for courage, and also for strength and activity..." They were each willing to look fear in the face and step into action despite this fear. Additionally, they each understood the power available when they activated their physical bodies to fight their foe. We possess a similar power over Satan when we physically and biochemically activate our bodies.

"They were men who were true at all times in whatsoever thing they were entrusted..." Each young man acted as a true 'man' by magnifying his stewardship and completing each assignment given. They kept their promises at all times.

"They were men of truth and soberness..." A key part of sobriety is maintaining our honesty and truth with regard to every action. We are authentic with others when we are willing to be open and humble. We are willing to maintain a spirit of truth at all times including when we fall and lose important battles.

"They had been taught to keep the commandments of God..." Each of these young men knew and honored God's commandments. They did not pick which commandments they would keep and which they would ignore. They obeyed with exactness.

Consider the following verses, which further demonstrate qualities possessed by the sons of Helaman:

> *45 And now I say unto you, my beloved brother Moroni, that never had I seen so great courage, nay, not amongst all the Nephites.*
>
> *46 For as I had ever called them my sons (for they were all of them very young) even so they said unto me: Father, behold our God is with us, and he will not suffer that we should fall; then let us go forth; we would not slay our brethren if they would let us alone; therefore let us go, lest they should overpower the army of Antipus.*
>
> *47 Now they never had fought, yet they did not fear death; and they did think more upon the liberty of their fathers than they did upon their lives; yea, they had been taught by their mothers, that if they did not doubt, God would deliver them.*
> *– Alma 56:45-47*

Each of these young men were able to stand firm in their decision to fight for their purpose even though they had never fought before and had no experience in how to defeat their enemy. They exhibited perfect faith in those who had stewardship over them and in the power of God to deliver them. That trust transcended their own fear of death or demise.

Have you ever been asked by a mentor or leader to take specific steps towards self-mastery that you didn't like or feared would be too difficult? In these moments of feeling inexperience and inadequacy, are you willing to trust in their counsel and do exactly what they say without shrinking to the fear of possible failure?

Fearing God Over Men

Moroni exemplifies another key quality of a successful warrior:

> *28 Yea, behold I do not fear your power nor*
> *your authority, but it is my God whom I fear;*
> *and it is according to his commandments that*
> *I do take my sword to defend the cause of my*
> *country...*
> *– Alma 60:28*

Moroni was a man stripped of pride and ego. He did not allow the opinions of men to influence his beliefs or actions.

He was far more concerned with the commandments given to him by God.

Pahoran, the political leader of the Nephite people exhibited similar humility in his answer to Moroni's epistle censuring him for not sending men and supplies to the battlefront.

> *9 And now, in your epistle you have censured me, but it mattereth not; I am not angry, but do rejoice in the greatness of your heart. I, Pahoran, do not seek for power, save only to retain my judgment-seat that I may preserve the rights and the liberty of my people. My soul standeth fast in that liberty in the which God hath made us free.*
> *– Alma 61:9*

Exactness in Obedience

Perhaps the most important quality of a successful warrior was exhibited by the sons of Helaman during a critical battle.

> *19 But behold, my little band of two thousand and sixty fought most desperately; yea, they were firm before the Lamanites, and did administer death unto all those who opposed them.*

20 And as the remainder of our army were about to give way before the Lamanites, behold, those two thousand and sixty were firm and undaunted.

21 Yea, and they did obey and observe to perform every word of command with exactness; yea, and even according to their faith it was done unto them; and I did remember the words which they said unto me that their mothers had taught them.

22 And now behold, it was these my sons, and those men who had been selected to convey the prisoners, to whom we owe this great victory; for it was they who did beat the Lamanites; therefore they were driven back to the city of Manti.

25 And it came to pass that there were two hundred, out of my two thousand and sixty, who had fainted because of the loss of blood; nevertheless, according to the goodness of God, and to our great astonishment, and also the joy of our whole army, there was not one soul of them who did perish; yea, and neither was there one soul among them who had not received many wounds.

26 And now, their preservation was astonishing to our whole army, yea, that they should be spared while there was a thousand of our brethren who were slain. And we do justly ascribe it to the miraculous power of God, because of their exceeding faith in that which they had been taught to believe—that there was a just God, and whosoever did not doubt, that they should be preserved by his marvelous power.

27 Now this was the faith of these of whom I have spoken; they are young, and their minds are firm, and they do put their trust in God continually.
– Alma 57:19-22, 25-27

When we obey every command from our leaders and from God with exactness, we unlock a principle of power. Exactness in obedience can mean the difference between receiving the promised blessing of deliverance or losing it. "I, the Lord, am bound when ye do what I say; but when ye do not what I say, ye have no promise" (D&C 82:10). There are moments when 'close' can mean the difference between lighting the fire of transformation or leaving logs that lay dormant because we didn't put forth sufficient energy required by exactness.

There is a major difference between exactness and perfection. We may obey with exactness and still make mistakes. Life is full of learning opportunities that may result in a temporary failure or defeat.

Exactness is an attitude of sharpness in obedience. It is the opposite of slothfulness. It includes the willingness to be proactive rather than always being compelled to obey.

During subsequent times of peace, the Nephites demonstrated the prosperity, peace and safety that can result from exactness in obedience.

> *30 Yea, and there was continual peace among them, and exceedingly great prosperity in the church because of their heed and diligence which they gave unto the word of God, which was declared unto them by Helaman, and Shiblon, and Corianton, and Ammon and his brethren, yea, and by all those who had been ordained by the holy order of God, being baptized unto repentance, and sent forth to preach among the people.*
> *– Alma 49:30*

The Gift of Prophecy

A powerful gift utilized by Captain Moroni during the battle with Zarahemnah is available to each of us in our respective areas of stewardship. Consider the following verses:

> *22 Behold, now it came to pass that they durst not come against the Nephites in the borders of Jershon; therefore they departed out of the land of Antionum into the wilderness, and took their journey round about in the wilderness, away by the head of the river Sidon, that they might come into the land of Manti and take possession of the land; for they did not suppose that the armies of Moroni would know whither they had gone.*

> *23 But it came to pass, as soon as they had departed into the wilderness Moroni sent spies into the wilderness to watch their camp; and Moroni, also, knowing of the prophecies of Alma, sent certain men unto him, desiring him that he should inquire of the Lord whither the armies of the Nephites should go to defend themselves against the Lamanites.*

24 And it came to pass that the word of the Lord came unto Alma, and Alma informed the messengers of Moroni, that the armies of the Lamanites were marching round about in the wilderness, that they might come over into the land of Manti, that they might commence an attack upon the weaker part of the people. And those messengers went and delivered the message unto Moroni.
– Alma 43: 22-24

Just like Alma, we can draw upon the powerful gift of prophecy to know where Satan will attempt to attack. This is a gift of the Spirit that can be a privilege for everyone who is a covenant disciple of Jesus Christ over their areas of stewardship.

Prophesying is far different than just predicting, but predicting can be a good start as we mentioned previously. Prophesying requires that we establish a connection with God. It requires asking a question which may be something like, "How will Satan attempt to defeat me today? What will be his exact technique and timing of attack?" It requires our willingness to quietly listen to the whispering of the Spirit with the humility to take action when the answer comes.

With this gift, an individual can receive revelation regarding the exact time, place and circumstances of Satan's attack. He or she can then plan by drilling all necessary actions required to win the anticipated battle.

Mighty Prayer

In Alma 46, Captain Moroni prayed three times in quick succession. In verse 13 "he prayed mightily", in verse 16 "Moroni prayed" and in verse 17, "he poured out his soul to God." Check yourself. Does this sound like the way you pray? Is your urgency to win your battles similar to Moroni's?

In my experience as a therapist, I have observed a fascinating and scary complacency about winning the war for self-mastery including sexual self-mastery. I read once what it is like to talk to someone who is freezing to death. They enter a type of delirium that makes them feel unconcerned.

Satan has found a similar way to influence brain chemistry when it comes to self-mastery. This influence disconnects us from our power source, and we likely find ourselves "freezing to death." As we do, we may notice a similar complacency and find our communication with God losing the urgency that Moroni demonstrated.

An Attitude of Prevention

Over and over again, the Nephites learned the painful lesson that adequately protecting their cities is far easier and less costly than having to recover a lost one. From their places of safety, they could easily defeat the enemy without the loss of a single life.

9 And now as Moroni had supposed that there should be men sent to the city of Nephihah, to the assistance of the people to maintain that city, and knowing that it was easier to keep the city from falling into the hands of the Lamanites than to retake it from them, he supposed that they would easily maintain that city.

10 Therefore he retained all his force to maintain those places which he had recovered.

11 And now, when Moroni saw that the city of Nephihah was lost he was exceedingly sorrowful, and began to doubt, because of the wickedness of the people, whether they should not fall into the hands of their brethren.

12 Now this was the case with all his chief captains. They doubted and marveled also because of the wickedness of the people, and this because of the success of the Lamanites over them.

13 And it came to pass that Moroni was angry with the government, because of their indifference concerning the freedom of their country.
– Alma 59:9-13

Likewise, preventing addiction and self-mastery challenges is far easier than recovering from a lost battle. Prevention requires preparation. It requires developing a keen awareness of the enemy and of his tactics. It requires building adequate protective borders against possible attacks.

Our greatest vulnerability in the preventive battle is indifference and slothfulness. Satan is expert in bringing us to a state of indifference by the lack of an attack and a long period of apparent peace. He lulls us into a sense of carnal security to the degree that we may forget his diabolical methods of attack. We may forget to close our gates of protection, and we may even forget why we needed walls in the first place. He then launches a "surprise attack" when we least expect it and drags us back into the yoke of bondage if we aren't prepared.

Indifference to prevention can ultimately lead to a lost battle and to lost ground that must then be recovered.

Knowing Why You Are Fighting...And Write It Down

Captain Moroni exhibited the quality of knowing why he was fighting and then writing it down. In Alma 46:12, the first action he takes as a leader is to write down why he is fighting. He doesn't just hold it in his head. Those who are in our Sons of Helaman, Men of Moroni or Eternal Warriors Training programs know that this is where Question One in the Captain's log comes from: "Why are you fighting? Why don't you just give up?"

A very common mistake for new Warriors is to think that holding these reasons in their head is enough. It is not. Write the reasons down. Pull them from inside your soul every day and write them down again. This is one of the most vital drills to do when fighting for self-mastery. Writing down two to five reasons each day is enough. It's okay if they are the same as yesterday. It's okay if they are different. Carry these with you all day. We prefer the simplicity of 3x5 cards.

From a purely psychology/science perspective, the human brain is like most vehicles.....it needs direction and fuel. Reviewing why you are fighting, first thing every day, gives the brain direction and fuel. Review the card(s) about six times throughout the day... More fuel, more direction.

We observe that we live on a planet that is a "lone and dreary" world. It is the same place where Satan was cast down. As part of our Eternal growth plan, we have been sent here to exercise our spiritual muscles against his opposition. Our daily earthly routine may feel like being in a spiritual weight room. Consider the following scenario.

A friend approaches you after going to the gym for a week or two with sadness and frustration in their voice.

"I really don't feel like I am making any difference."

As a good friend, you ask, "What do you mean?"

Your friend replies, "Every time I go to the gym, it feels like everything is against me. All I get is resistance to everything I do. I find myself doing the same thing over and over and over again!

And to top it off," your friend pauses and shows you two pictures on their phone, "I took a picture of the weight room before I started my workout today and I took a second picture after spending almost 2 hours there! Can't you see?! They look the same! Obviously, I am making no difference!"

We have been told that this life is a test. I am confident that part of that test is to see if we can figure out that this life is also a **Training** or a **Workout**. We are told in multiple revelations that we are preparing for a more advanced phase in the next life.

Many have learned the joy of the gym. They expect opposition. They expect repetition. They understand the experience of having almost unobservable, incremental growth. They understand that the goal is to make a difference inside of them, not so much the space around them.

And if you are ambitious enough to take on a personal trainer and/or you have ambitions to be one of the Noble and Great Ones of the Final Days, you know to expect a more than intense workout every day! These workouts, when taken seriously, can help you to build character and personalities similar to success warriors in the Book of Mormon.

Key Takeway From This Chapter

If we want to consistently win our battles, we can learn a tremendous amount from the most successful warriors in the Book of Mormon. They were men of sound integrity who didn't veer from their values and their training especially when a threat from the enemy was apparent. They dedicated their lives to staying in every battle until the enemy was vanquished.

CHAPTER 5

Successful Battle Strategies

As we examine the war chapters in Alma, we discover several battle strategies that always lead to victory. These strategies align us with God's infinite power and enable us to put on His protective armor. They help us to fight with a righteous and pure purpose. And, they help us to maintain a firm stand on the battlefield until victory is assured.

Many of the strategies outlined in Alma demonstrate a combined use of Spiritual and Behavioral principles. Quite often, when people first become aware of the idea of training or interventions that synchronize or synergize these two principles, they try to "force" a dichotomy. It's as if their challenging question is something like, "Are you teaching your people to work with God, or are you teaching them to fight by themselves?"

I have never been in a dangerous military situation, but, from what I understand, soldiers in combat have no problem combining the two principles. They pray with all their heart, might, mind and strength hoping desperately for the involvement of Divine power. But, then they fight with all their heart, might, mind and strength. If interviewed after a battle, they would tell us, "We and God both work full out during the battle. We can figure out who gets the credit after the dust settles. In the end, it doesn't matter who gets credit when we work as a team."

As we consider how to fully align with God while giving our all to the battle, we find several common themes outlined in the Book of Mormon.

We Fight With Our Savior, Jesus Christ

It isn't enough to have a cause that moves us when we only draw upon our own relative strength and experience. We fight against a vicious and unrelenting dark general who possesses at least 6,000 years of experience in defeating men and bringing them under the yoke of bondage.

The critical key to success in any battle we fight is to align ourselves with the absolute power of God and the redeeming power of the Atonement. The Atonement is infinite in its depth and breadth to empower and save. When we align ourselves with this power, we have unlimited capacity to win against any attack even when we may lack worldly experience to fight.

Consider the following examples from scripture where the Nephites' success in battle resulted from their connection to the Savior and his grace:

48 And it came to pass that when the men of Moroni saw the fierceness and the anger of the Lamanites, they were about to shrink and flee from them. And Moroni, perceiving their intent, sent forth and inspired their hearts with these thoughts—yea, the thoughts of their lands, their liberty, yea, their freedom from bondage.

49 And it came to pass that they turned upon the Lamanites, and they cried with one voice unto the Lord their God, for their liberty and their freedom from bondage.

50 And they began to stand against the Lamanites with power; and in that selfsame hour that they cried unto the Lord for their freedom, the Lamanites began to flee before them; and they fled even to the waters of Sidon.
– Alma 43:48-50

Here we see that the mere faithful cry for help was sufficient to turn the tide of a battle that was all but lost. Until that moment, the Nephites had been outnumbered and overpowered by the strength of their adversary. Their natural capabilities were no match for the Lamanites. Statistics would dictate that failure was imminent. But, the Nephites weren't counting on their natural capabilities to deliver them when they cried for help. They exercised faith in an unseen power and force that they felt confident could show them a way to victory where none was apparent.

What battles are you currently "losing?" Where does the adversary appear to have you pinned down or in full retreat? Are you able to trust in His power to provide you with sufficient strength and skill for victory? When was the last time that you asked for that power to deliver you and then held fast with the trust that it would come?

---

3 But now, ye behold that the Lord is with us; and ye behold that he has delivered you into our hands. And now I would that ye should understand that this is done unto us because of our religion and our faith in Christ. And now ye see that ye cannot destroy this our faith.

4 Now ye see that this is the true faith of God; yea, ye see that God will support, and keep, and preserve us, so long as we are faithful unto him, and unto our faith, and our religion; and never will the Lord suffer that we shall be destroyed except we should fall into transgression and deny our faith.
– Alma 44:3-4

In the preceding verses, Captain Moroni pointed out a critical part of drawing upon God's power. It is through our faith that we are saved from destruction. And, it is through our religion with its laws, covenants and ordinances that we can be cleansed and connected to God through Jesus Christ. As long as we remain faithful to those covenants, God will protect us from our enemies.

It may feel tempting to neglect important covenants when times are peaceful and flow with relative ease. Satan is cunning at convincing us that other things are more important and should take precedence in our mind and heart. However, the commandments and our covenants keep us in a state of connection with Eternal power. The strength of this connection can not generally be re-established instantaneously after being neglected for weeks, months or years. Like a rope woven strand by strand, each covenant faithfully kept will open our minds and hearts to greater flow of light and love and subsequently strengthen our ability to act from love rather than fear.

Do you feel like you're being continually overpowered by Satan's powerful waves of fear? Have you remembered the covenants that you have made or perhaps the ones that you have neglected to make because you feared the commitment? How faithfully do you honor them? Where could you step up your commitment?

And he said: Surely God shall not suffer that
we, who are despised because we take upon
us the name of Christ, shall be trodden down
and destroyed, until we bring it upon us by our
own transgressions.
– Alma 46:18

While we may feel derided on all sides because of our decision to be called by the name of Jesus Christ, this covenant relationship is the key to our safety and protection. Are we willing to bear His name in all situations? Do we fear the trends of the world more than the commandments given from the Savior by whose name we are called?

---

28 And it came to pass that the Nephites began
again to be victorious, and to reclaim their
rights and their privileges.

29 Many times did the Lamanites attempt
to encircle them about by night, but in these
attempts they did lose many prisoners.

30 And many times did they attempt to
administer of their wine to the Nephites, that
they might destroy them with poison or with
drunkenness.

31 But behold, the Nephites were not slow to remember the Lord their God in this their time of affliction. They could not be taken in their snares; yea, they would not partake of their wine, save they had first given to some of the Lamanite prisoners.
– Alma 55:28-31

In contrast to earlier defeats and bondage that stemmed from the Nephites' slothfulness to remember, as they sharpened their remembrance, they could detect every snare and attack from their adversaries. The Nephites enjoyed freedom when they were quick to remember their dependence on God.

Do Satan's snares regularly catch you unawares?

One of the objectives of our prevention and recovery programs is to help participants sharpen their spiritual senses and awareness of Satan's attacks long before he has had the opportunity to surround them in full hand-to-hand combat. As they draw upon God's power and remember what is important to them, they learn to see Satan coming from afar and become effective snipers to counter his attacks.

55 And now it came to pass that when they had surrendered themselves up unto us, behold, I numbered those young men who had fought with me, fearing lest there were many of them slain.

56 But behold, to my great joy, there had not one soul of them fallen to the earth; yea, and they had fought as if with the strength of God; yea, never were men known to have fought with such miraculous strength; and with such mighty power did they fall upon the Lamanites, that they did frighten them; and for this cause did the Lamanites deliver themselves up as prisoners of war.
– Alma 56:55-56

And similarly these verses:

10 Therefore we did pour out our souls in prayer to God, that he would strengthen us and deliver us out of the hands of our enemies, yea, and also give us strength that we might retain our cities, and our lands, and our possessions, for the support of our people.

11 Yea, and it came to pass that the Lord our God did visit us with assurances that he would deliver us; yea, insomuch that he did speak peace to our souls, and did grant unto us great faith, and did cause us that we should hope for our deliverance in him.

12 And we did take courage with our small force which we had received, and were fixed with a determination to conquer our enemies, and to maintain our lands, and our possessions, and our wives, and our children, and the cause of our liberty.

13 And thus we did go forth with all our might against the Lamanites, who were in the city of Manti...
– Alma 58:10-13

These verses demonstrate that statistical strength of numbers and natural capability does not matter when we are connected with Jesus Christ. His assurances of protection and safety are always backed with miraculous events that the faithless might call "luck" or "circumstance." It is my belief that God sometimes gives overwhelming statistics so that, in the end, we are assured that He is the one who delivered us versus our own wisdom and strength.

37 But, behold, it mattereth not—we trust God will deliver us, notwithstanding the weakness of our armies, yea, and deliver us out of the hands of our enemies.

39 And those sons of the people of Ammon, of whom I have so highly spoken, are with me in the city of Manti; and the Lord has supported them, yea, and kept them from falling by the sword, insomuch that even one soul has not been slain.

40 But behold, they have received many wounds; nevertheless they stand fast in that liberty wherewith God has made them free; and they are strict to remember the Lord their God from day to day; yea, they do observe to keep his statutes, and his judgments, and his commandments continually; and their faith is strong in the prophecies concerning that which is to come.
– Alma 58:37-40

From these verses, we can clearly see that aligning with the Savior is in no way passive. It requires continual diligence and exactness and doing all that He has commanded. We clearly demonstrate our alignment by our willingness to hearken especially when the commandment feels challenging for us to obey.

Captain Moroni shares the following perspective regarding our alignment with Jesus:

> *But now, ye behold that the Lord is with us;*
> *and ye behold that he has delivered you into*
> *our hands. And **now I would that ye should***
> ***understand that this is done unto us because***
> ***of our religion and our faith in Christ**. And*
> *now we see that ye cannot destroy this our*
> *faith.*
> *– Alma 44:3*

When Captain Moroni gives all the credit to Jesus Christ, he is not erasing the hard work that he and his men exerted towards becoming skilled, strong and dedicated. He is reminding his men and his enemy that the power to win comes from the combined effort we make with the Father, Jesus Christ and the Holy Ghost.

We play a role for our warriors like that played by Captain Moroni in his community. In our training sessions, we drill and drill and drill how to increase discernment (detecting the enemy early), followed by high speed, accurate and strong responses. Just like Captain Moroni, we, of course, obtain and maintain a working relationship with God, but we don't expect to win our battles without doing our best part.

Each of the above accounts from Alma are very clear. When we fight with the Savior and bring our very best to the fight, we always have sufficient power and resources for victory.

We Fight for What We Love

We cannot truly feel committed to a purposeful cause when we simply resist Satan and his attacks out of fear, anger or hatred. This motivation might be okay to get the fire of action started, but is inadequate to win the war long-term. Being continually motivated by fear, anger and/or hatred can lead to further captivity.

Our commitment has more depth and enduring force when we fight for what we love. Captain Moroni exemplified this love during the battle with Zarahemnah and in numerous other battles:

> *And it came to pass that they did stop and withdrew a pace from them. And Moroni said unto Zerahemnah: Behold, Zerahemnah, that we do not desire to be men of blood. Ye know that ye are in our hands, yet we do not desire to slay you.*
> *– Alma 44:1*

Moroni clearly abhorred the shedding of blood, yet his love for the liberty of his people superseded his own life. When required to defend that liberty, he would take the life of another only if absolutely necessary.

When we examine many of Captain Moroni's characteristics, we see a man motivated by love for God, for his people and even for his enemies whom he did not joy in harming. Consider again these verses:

> *11 And Moroni was a strong and a mighty man; he was a man of a perfect understanding; yea, a man that did not delight in bloodshed; a man whose soul did joy in the liberty and the freedom of his country, and his brethren from bondage and slavery;*
>
> *12 Yea, a man whose heart did swell with thanksgiving to his God, for the many privileges and blessings which he bestowed upon his people; a man who did labor exceedingly for the welfare and safety of his people.*
>
> *13 Yea, and he was a man who was firm in the faith of Christ, and he had sworn with an oath to defend his people, his rights, and his country, and his religion, even to the loss of his blood.*
> *– Alma 48:11-13*

Many young men who enter our sexual addiction recovery programs aren't necessarily motivated by love when they first enter the program. Many are primarily afraid of social rejection. However, as they progress, they connect with moments somewhere in their past where they have experienced at least one loving, bonding moment with God. Even in the pit of despair, that sensation doesn't go away. Because they've tried living in the "great and spacious building," the awareness that God loves them can ultimately motivate them to shift direction.

What is your current motivation for change? Is it primarily rooted in shame, frustration or anger? Do you feel like you just want to cut something undesirable out of your life?

There was a time in my life when I felt really dissatisfied with my current career and job. After many months of searching for a change, I was unable to have any success. One day, a friend and senior co-worker contacted me and asked about my desires and my discontent. During the conversation, he shared a powerful insight that changed my life. He said, "Reuben, if you're running away from something, everything else will look good. If you really want long-term success and satisfaction, you need to figure out WHAT YOU ARE RUNNING TOWARDS."

In our programs, we regularly ask our participants to consider, "What are you fighting for?" We don't ask them to focus on "what they are fighting against." Our goal is to help them connect with something that they love far more than any secondary benefits that their self-mastery challenge may bring.

When we connect with what we love, we find a passion and motivation that has staying power. We find a deep heartfelt reason to stay in the battle until we win.

We Draw a Firm Line in the Sand on Our Standards

Nephite leaders like Captain Moroni and the men of Antipus exemplified another key fighting strategy by standing their ground relentlessly. Moroni demonstrated this strategy when he refused to negotiate terms with the enemy. Notice from the following verses how Moroni drew a firm line in the sand and would not allow the enemy to cross that line.

> *10 And now when Zerahemnah had made an end of speaking these words, Moroni returned the sword and the weapons of war, which he had received, unto Zerahemnah, saying: Behold, we will end the conflict.*

> *11 Now I cannot recall the words which I have spoken, therefore as the Lord liveth, ye shall not depart except ye depart with an oath that ye will not return again against us to war. Now as ye are in our hands we will spill your blood*

upon the ground, or ye shall submit to the
conditions which I have proposed.
– Alma 44:10-11

Moroni also demonstrated this quality when writing to Ammoron in which he set conditions for prisoner exchange and which Ammoron rejected for a lesser condition. These were Moroni's conditions:

11 ...therefore I will close my epistle by telling
you that I will not exchange prisoners, save it
be on conditions that ye will deliver up a man
and his wife and his children, for one prisoner;
if this be the case that ye will do it, I will
exchange.

12 And behold, if ye do not this, I will come
against you with my armies; yea, even I will
arm my women and my children, and I will
come against you, and I will follow you even
into your own land, which is the land of our
first inheritance; yea, and it shall be blood
for blood, yea, life for life; and I will give you
battle even until you are destroyed from off the
face of the earth.
– Alma 54:11-12

When these conditions were rejected by Ammoron, Moroni remained true to his word including arming the women and children being held captive by the Lamanites.

It is also important to note that setting firm standards for ourselves and maintaining them results in greater liberty and freedom than living in a state of sloppiness with lower standards. Consider the liberty that the people of Nephi enjoyed when they planted a firm standard in their lives:

> *And it came to pass also that he caused the*
> *title of liberty to be hoisted upon every tower*
> *which was in all the land, which was possessed*
> *by the Nephites; and thus Moroni planted the*
> *standard of liberty among the Nephites.*
> *– Alma 46:36*

The Title of Liberty turned the tide of evil that was instigated by Amalackiah. It helped to draw a firm line in the sand by which the Nephites rejected Amalackiah's plan for domination.

It may seem counterintuitive, but when we get stuck in daily survival mode, the quickest way out of the chaos and feeling overwhelmed is to set and maintain clear standards. During challenging moments, we may feel tempted to rationalize our way out of those standards, but they secure a pathway to freedom and victory.

And, it's important that we decide the standards by which we will live. A common question that men ask when they are recovering from addiction is, 'What exactly defines a lost battle?' They are totally surprised when I tell them that they get to decide. They're surprised that someone else isn't going to clarify the ambiguity. I have discovered that giving them too much clarity actually makes them less committed to winning. By allowing them to decide upon the standard by which they will judge a lost battle, they draw a firmer line in the sand.

We are sometimes criticized for the intensity of our training techniques in the programs that we offer. Some disagree that we are not at war with a real enemy. But, we have found that when someone doesn't accept that they are in a life or death situation, that individual lacks sufficient sharpness to hold their ground and overcome their challenges.

We have found that an individual will compromise his or her standards when they buy into a lie or some kind of limiting belief about themselves or about others. Buying into the lie gives Satan a way to tempt them with a way to experience momentary relief from the pain or fear they are now experiencing. If the individual doesn't find a way to reconnect with his or her values quickly, Satan then influences them into a rationalization as to why this one time can be an exception. My wife, Tina, calls this, "Looking for our permission slip to fail." When individuals buy into this thinking, they will find themselves caving once again to a behavioral pattern that they would not have chosen when connected to their values.

One of the most powerful tools that we use with clients to help them catch lies and limiting beliefs is called the Lost Battle Analysis. It is similar to an After-Action Review but it involves analyzing how the individual became trapped in a Satanic Spin™ by walking through the Spin backwards from the moment of deciding to act against their values to the moment when they were first "flashed" by the lie. This process helps them to identify the exact lie that initiated the Spin. They can then choose to replace that lie with a new truth.

In one of my Sons of Helaman addiction recovery groups, a young man who had succeeded in winning against addictive behaviors for five consecutive weeks subsequently succumbed twice in a seven day period and was required to start over in his progression. As the group reviewed what had occurred in a Lost Battle Analysis, it was observed by me and this young man's fellow warriors that his resolve lacked the intensity exhibited when one truly holds his ground. This young man began to understand that, when really bad people are trying to hurt you and your loved ones, the smallest decrease in vigilance could lead to destruction. He recognized that he lacked an intense, ferocious plan. He was too passive, and when the time came to stand his ground, he gave in to the enemy's tactics.

Change doesn't necessarily occur immediately once the new truth is identified. But, persistence in noticing and catching Satan's lie either before or after a lost battle will help the individual to find liberation through new truths that they choose to believe. The more that we recognize the enemy's attacks through the lies that he attempts to plant, the easier it becomes to draw a firm line in the sand and hold fast to truth.

We Fight With a Firm Determination That Excludes Retreat

Antipus and his men exhibited an important quality of how we should fight through their fierce determination to maintain their cause. This decision excluded retreat. They would fight or die in the process as demonstrated by the following verses:

> *15 And these are the cities which they possessed when I arrived at the city of Judea; and I found Antipus and his men toiling with their might to fortify the city.*
>
> *16 Yea, and they were depressed in body as well as in spirit, for they had fought valiantly by day and toiled by night to maintain their cities; and thus they had suffered great afflictions of every kind.*
>
> *17 And now they were determined to conquer in this place or die; therefore you may well suppose that this little force which I brought with me, yea, those sons of mine, gave them great hopes and much joy.*
> *– Alma 56:15-17*

There are times when it is appropriate to adjust the goals and aspirations that we have set. But, there are also times that we need to burn our boats and bridges of retreat and decide to "conquer or die." This kind of determination generally elevates our commitment and ferocity to the degree that we take total responsibility for our lives and vigorously stop the retreat.

Constantly 'caving' when a challenge feels hard will never result in a transformative change. As we've pointed out before, It's like rubbing two sticks together with the intention to make fire but neglecting to do so hard enough and long enough to see the ignition occur. Fire can transform only at the moment of ignition. Getting close to ignition with a good effort was commendable, but it didn't produce any noticeable results.

We Put on the Whole Armor of God

The way in which the Nephites showed up for battle demonstrated the importance of putting on the **whole armor of God** to fully defend and protect ourselves from the adversary.

> *18 And it came to pass that he (Moroni) met the Lamanites in the borders of Jershon, and his people were armed with swords, and with cimeters, and all manner of weapons of war.*

19 And when the armies of the Lamanites saw that the people of Nephi, or that Moroni, had prepared his people with breastplates and with arm-shields, yea, and also shields to defend their heads, and also they were dressed with thick clothing...
– Alma 43:18 - 19

In their fully armored position, the Nephites were able to protect themselves and effectively defeat their adversary.

38 While on the other hand, there was now and then a man fell among the Nephites, by their swords and the loss of blood, they being shielded from the more vital parts of the body, or the more vital parts of the body being shielded from the strokes of the Lamanites, by their breastplates, and their armshields, and their head-plates; and thus the Nephites did carry on the work of death among the Lamanites.
– Alma 43:38

In our haste to tackle our daily challenges, it can feel tempting to neglect key pieces of our armor. We may also find ourselves trying to be 'efficient' in girding ourselves properly and ensuring that we are properly protected. Being 'efficient' can be helpful in many aspects of our lives, but it doesn't generally work when we are training to use a sword and shield effectively or when we are ensuring that our spiritual breastplates, arm shields and headplates are fully buckled and secure.

Putting on the whole armor of God requires thoughtfulness. It requires our full attention. It requires our willingness to go beyond checking the boxes of scripture reading, daily prayer and church attendance.

Here are some of the many different ways to put on the full armor of God and protect ourselves in modern Spiritual/ Psychological Warfare.

- Prayer can be used as both a weapon and a protection.

- Reading and Audio recording – When you are adding quality information to your brain through your eyes and/or your ears, it blocks much of the input from the Dark Side.

- Gratitude – through journals or direct messaging. When we are focusing on what is and has made our lives better, it leaves less mental and emotional space for unedifying thoughts and feelings.

- Friends and family – Being with, being accountable to, working with, playing with others makes us less vulnerable. Satan and his demons are like cats of prey. They strive to isolate their victims.

- Securing electronic devices and staying away from dangerous places – While internet security/blocking tools have merit, it is unwise to rely on them. Remember, in most cases, the best defense is a good offense. If you are intentionally doing Good, you are highly unlikely to do Bad at the same time.

We Go on the Offensive and Strike Back

Consider the following verses and an effective battle strategy that they demonstrate:

> 36 And it came to pass that the Lamanites, when they saw **the Nephites coming upon them in their rear**, turned them about and began to contend with the army of Lehi.
>
> 37 And **the work of death commenced on both sides**, but it was more dreadful on the part of the Lamanites, for their nakedness was exposed to the **heavy blows of the Nephites with their swords and their cimeters**, which brough death almost at every stroke.
> – Alma 43:36-37

There are several principles to observe here that are a bit different than the current, traditional interventions used in addiction recovery and self-mastery. Notice that the Nephites are on the offensive during the battle. Yes, the Lamanites are in the lands of the Nephites, but the Nephites don't wait to be hit first. It is important that we do not wait for the attacks. We need to hit with **Good** actions before the dark side hits with darkness, torment or temptation.

Next, observe that the intensity level of the battle is significant. Many warriors are surprised at the ferocity of the battle. We may hit our enemy with a thought, a feeling or an action, and Satan's demons will likely hit back. In training like that done in our programs, we learn to break down these back and forth exchanges the same way one would in basketball, wrestling or fencing. With training and a skilled Psychological/Spiritual self-mastery trainer, an individual can gain greater skills in how to effectively 'hit back.'

Notice too that the Nephites used weapons that were relevant to their day. We have weapons today too. Weapons to not only protect and defend ourselves, but weapons to attack. Attacking includes going out of your way to do good.

Notice from the above verse that the Nephites hit with "heavy blows". They were not wimpy and "sweet." We teach concepts like "mother bear chemistry" (This is the feeling that mothers have when their children are threatened) and "Warrior Chemistry™" (the spontaneous feeling that a man has when his wife, family and home are threatened). No one ever wants to experience these intense sensations, but God blessed us with this significant capacity as needed. In Book of Mormon days, it was used on the outside of the body to fight battles with weapons held in one's hands. Now the battle primarily takes place inside the mind and body.

One of the most powerful weapons that we can use to "crush Satan's head" is our electronic devices. We can send a single message to a single person designed to uplift, encourage and empower, or we can do the same with large numbers of people through social media. For example, if Satan and/or some of his demons choose to mess with me for any obnoxious length of time, I will take out my tablet or phone, plug into the Holy Ghost and write something uplifting and helpful. Sometimes I'll attach a picture or a meme to it. Sometimes I attach a link or two to it. Then, as I think about the fifty thousand or more people it is about to go out to, I imagine looking at the Dark Side and think (with a nice portion of Warrior Chemistry), "You should not have messed with me (and my team)." Then I press "post" and visualize the ripple effect on the thousands that it effects. It used to be just 10 or 20 people that would read it, but it grew line upon line, just like your contributions can.

Never underestimate the impact you have when you "hit back" at any level. We all have many memories of single moments with a single person that had a major impact on us that the giver may never realize how they influenced us. Start somewhere. Start now.

As you weigh how to appropriately strike back, also consider the following verses:

40 And they were pursued by Lehi and his men; and they were driven by Lehi into the waters of Sidon, and they crossed the waters of Sidon. And Lehi retained his armies upon the bank of the river Sidon that they should not cross.

41 And it came to pass that Moroni and his army met the Lamanites in the valley, on the other side of the river Sidon, and began to fall upon them and to slay them.

42 And the Lamanites did flee again before them towards the land of Manti; and they were met again by the armies of Moroni.
– Alma 43:40-42

These words and phrases, "pursued", "driven", "fall upon them", "slay them", "again" seem like words and phrases that would be used to describe the Lamanites attack on the Nephites, but actually, these are all words and phrases describing Lehi and Moroni and their warriors. We have been taught and trained all our lives to be nice, kind and meek. These words and phrases can make it sound like Moroni and his warriors were blood-thirsty, but they were not. They understood that they were dealing with a dedicated, intelligent and ferocious enemy that was willing to destroy them and their families.

Perhaps Satan learned something from the Book of Mormon days and has strategically changed his methods. Perhaps he realizes that a war which is easy to be seen with the eyes is too easy for us to win. It is too easy for us to know who the enemy is and for us to experience intense responses. Perhaps he has changed his tactics to the more subtle psychological methods that are so subtle that most of us mistake his words in our minds as "Negative Self-Talk" and don't recognize any war being waged at all.

What we learn from these verses is that we need to maintain a vigilance that borders on ruthlessness. We need to have the mentality, not as much about avoiding evil, but doing Good again and again in order to maintain dominance in the Spiritual and Psychological war.

We Team up With Other Warriors

When he raised the Title of Liberty, Captain Moroni courageously shares his hopes at risk of being mocked and rejected. He knew his ability to fight the enemy would be stronger if he brought fellow warriors together.

This has been one of my (Maurice's) most important discoveries in my adult life. I am naturally an introvert. I prefer to be by myself or in very small groups of two. But as I have progressed, I have discovered that I need to create and be on teams, both to win psychological/spiritual/behavioral wars and to build mountain-moving/Red-Sea-parting Passion

Projects. The organization, Life Changing Services, is one of those projects, a set of Warrior teams, made up of men and women, who have gathered under a "Title of Liberty," or a set of common goals. We bring our individual talents and spiritual gifts, and we synchronize them with each other and our God and His team, to serve the world.

In deciding who to add to your team, consider the following:

- What are you fighting for?

- Who would be a good member on your team?

- Share your Title of Liberty with others and invite them to fight side by side with you. Social Media works really well for this.

Key Takeaway From This Chapter

The Nephites demonstrated over and over that, in order to defeat an ominous enemy who relentlessly attacks, we must align ourselves with Jesus Christ and his infinite power, fight for what we love, draw a firm line in the sand with standards, execute with a firm determination that excludes retreat and put on the whole armour of God. We must be ready to strike back with good rather than always being on the defense and strike with ferociousness and great strength. And, it's important that we never try to win without the strength of our fellow mortal warriors.

CHAPTER 6

Protecting Our Wins and Gaining Further Ground

As we fight the war for self-mastery, we learn important principles from Nephite captains about how to protect the ground that we've won and win further ground. It starts with protecting our borders with strong defenses. And, it requires that our strongest fortifications are placed in the weakest areas of our self-mastery to protect us against attack.

Consider what can be learned about this concept from the following sets of verses:

> *7 Now it came to pass that while Amalickiah had thus been obtaining power by fraud and deceit, Moroni, on the other hand, had been preparing the minds of the people to be faithful unto the Lord their God.*

> *8 Yea, he had been strengthening the armies of the Nephites, and erecting small forts, or places of resort; throwing up banks of earth round about to enclose his armies, and also building*

walls of stone to encircle them about, round about their cities and the borders of their lands; yea, all round about the land.

9 And in their weakest fortifications he did place the greater number of men; and thus he did fortify and strengthen the land which was possessed by the Nephites.

10 And thus he was preparing to support their liberty, their lands, their wives, and their children, and their peace, and that they might live unto the Lord their God, and that they might maintain that which was called by their enemies the cause of Christians.
– Alma 48:7-10

Also, observe what occurred in each instance where weak cities were fortified:

5 Now at this time the chief captains of the Lamanites were astonished exceedingly, because of the wisdom of the Nephites in preparing their places of security.
– Alma 49:5

14 But behold, to their astonishment, the city of Noah, which had hitherto been a weak

place, had now, by the means of Moroni,
become strong, yea, even to exceed the strength
of the city Ammonihah.
– Alma 49:14

18 Now behold, the Lamanites could not get
into their forts of security by any other way
save by the entrance, because of the highness of
the bank which had been thrown up, and the
depth of the ditch which had been dug round
about, save it were by the entrance.

19 And thus were the Nephites prepared to
destroy all such as should attempt to climb up
to enter the fort by any other way, by casting
over stones and arrows at them.

20 Thus they were prepared, yea, a body of
their strongest men, with their swords and
their slings, to smite down all who should
attempt to come into their place of security
by the place of entrance; and thus were they
prepared to defend themselves against the
Lamanites.
– Alma 49:18-20

When proper fortifications are in place, not only will the
enemy, in many cases, retreat but, when he does attack, Satan

can be easily defeated without resulting casualties on our part. In the ensuing verse, because of their preparations we see that the Nephites were able to defeat their enemy without a single casualty:

> *23 Thus the Nephites had all power over their enemies; and thus the Lamanites did attempt to destroy the Nephites until their chief captains were all slain; yea, and more than a thousand of the Lamanites were slain; while, on the other hand, there was not a single soul of the Nephites which was slain.*
> *– Alma 49:23*

Once we win new ground in the war for self-mastery, it is common to forget to maintain the very defenses that protected us and enabled us to win. For example, we may be succeeding with the support of a mentor, therapist or coach, but as soon as we begin to gain significant ground, we may choose to revert to fighting on our own. In this case, nothing had been firmly established for our long-term support and success.

Consider Captain Moroni's tactics for holding ground in the following verses:

> *25 Now Moroni, leaving a part of his army in the land of Jershon, lest by any means a part of the Lamanites should come into that land and take possession of the city, took the remaining*

*part of his army and marched over into the
land of Manti.*

*26 And he caused that all the people in that
quarter of the land should gather themselves
together to battle against the Lamanites, to
defend their lands and their country, their
rights and their liberties; therefore they were
prepared against the time of the coming of the
Lamanites.*
– Alma 43:25-26

And, also in this verse:

*15 Therefore, come unto me speedily with a
few of your men, and leave the remainder in
the charge of Lehi and Teancum; give unto
them power to conduct the war in that part of
the land, according to the Spirit of God, which
is also the spirit of freedom which is in them.*
– Alma 61:15

These verses demonstrate that, when we begin to win, it is
critical that we maintain the defenses of those areas that
enabled us to win in the first place. If we choose to become
slothful in maintaining our defenses, we choose to allow our
enemy a pathway into our kingdom.

The following verses demonstrate that, following a great

victory, Moroni took action to further fortify all of his cities rather than rest on his achievements:

> *1 And now it came to pass that Moroni did not stop making preparations for war, or to defend his people against the Lamanites; for he caused that his armies should commence in the commencement of the twentieth year of the reign of the judges, that they should commence in digging up heaps of earth round about all the cities, throughout all the land which was possessed by the Nephites.*
>
> *2 And upon the top of these ridges of earth he caused that there should be timbers, yea, works of timbers built up to the height of a man, round about the cities.*
>
> *3 And he caused that upon those works of timbers there should be a frame of pickets built upon the timbers round about; and they were strong and high.*
>
> *4 And he caused towers to be erected that overlooked those works of pickets, and he caused places of security to be built upon those towers, that the stones and the arrows of the Lamanites could not hurt them.*

5 And they were prepared that they could cast stones from the top thereof, according to their pleasure and their strength, and slay him who should attempt to approach near the walls of the city.
– Alma 50:1-5

We've heard many individuals recovering from an addiction say, "I just want to be done with this." Their implication seems to be that, once they've won their recovery battles, they can return to the life they once knew. But this isn't true. The war for self-mastery must be fought every single day for the rest of our lives. Satan has a relentless intention to destroy the very best and finest leaders of God's armies. His goal is to pursue us relentlessly until we are his. "When will the Lamanites stop attacking the Nephites? When every Nephite is dead."

Like Ammoron, Satan is also constantly looking for a way to "draw away a part of our forces" and to distract us in a way that he can defeat us.

13 And thus he was endeavoring to harass the Nephites, and to draw away a part of their forces to that part of the land, while he had commanded those whom he had left to possess the cities which he had taken, that they should also harass the Nephites on the borders by the east sea, and should take possession of

their lands as much as it was in their power,
according to the power of their armies.
– Alma 52:13

We learn another important lesson from Moroni in how he chose to maintain the cities that he won. He didn't just fortify those cities that were in his possession. He took initiative and examined all of the possible places of attack. He then cleared out any possible dangers posed by the Lamanites that could result in a break in his line of protection.

11 And thus he cut off all the strongholds of
the Lamanites in the east wilderness, yea, and
also on the west, fortifying the line between
the Nephites and the Lamanites, between the
land of Zarahemla and the land of Nephi, from
the west sea, running by the head of the river
Sidon—the Nephites possessing all the land
northward, yea, even all the land which was
northward of the land Bountiful, according to
their pleasure.

12 Thus Moroni, with his armies, which did
increase daily because of the assurance of
protection which his works did bring forth
unto them, did seek to cut off the strength and
the power of the Lamanites from off the lands
of their possessions, that they should have no

power upon the lands of their possession.
– Alma 50:11-12

Where are the possible breaks in your line of safety? What are you doing to notice them and fortify them from possible attack?

One final tactic that Moroni teaches us is that of pacing ourselves in gaining new ground. We may not be in a position to take new ground with our current resources. In these moments, we can choose to pause on gaining new ground and focus on fortifying the ground that we have successfully taken.

> *7 And it came to pass that he did no more*
> *attempt a battle with the Lamanites in that*
> *year, but he did employ his men in preparing for*
> *war, yea, and in making fortifications to guard*
> *against the Lamanites, yea, and also delivering*
> *their women and their children from famine*
> *and affliction, and providing food for their*
> *armies.*
> *– Alma 53:7*

There is another important lesson each of us learns as we grow from greater to greater light, awareness and self-mastery. As we gain more ground, we cross an important line from unawareness and neutrality into the Savior's camp. From that moment forward, we can't go back to neutrality. If we choose to leave the light we've once known, we may choose a fate similar to those who dissented from the Nephites:

> *36 Now these dissenters, having the same instruction and the same information of the Nephites, yea, having been instructed in the same knowledge of the Lord, nevertheless, it is strange to relate, not long after their dissensions they became more hardened and impenitent, and more wild, wicked and ferocious than the Lamanites—drinking in with the traditions of the Lamanites; giving way to indolence, and all manner of lasciviousness; yea, entirely forgetting the Lord their God.*
> *– Alma 47:36*

Key Takeaway From This Chapter

In our quest for new ground in the self-mastery battle, it is critical that we do not neglect the ground that we have won. Further, we must sufficiently strengthen that ground by remaining vigilant and by giving proper resources to all that we have won.

CHAPTER 7

Our Greatest Threat

Time and again, the Nephites demonstrated that our greatest threat to success is the threat from within. We are not our own worst enemy. Those around us are not our enemy. However, Satan is constantly working to convince us that we are the enemy and that those on our team are our enemies.

Divisions from within enable Satan to succeed in conquering our once strong places that have suffered from neglect. This neglect results when we shift our energy towards fighting our fellow warriors and holding a lack of forgiveness for them.

> *21 And we see that these promises have been*
> *verified to the people of Nephi; for it has been*
> *their quarrelings and their contentions, yea,*
> *their murderings, and their plunderings,*
> *their idolatry, their whoredoms, and their*
> *abominations, which were among themselves,*
> *which brought upon them their wars and their*
> *destructions.*
> *– Alma 50:21*

At numerous critical moments, the Nephites lost ground due to internal contentions. In fact, every war fought in the book of Alma began with dissensions, first from the Nehors, then from the Zoramites and later from Amalackiah, a Nephite dissenter.

We also read the account of the contention between the land of Lehi and the land of Morianton in Alma 50 and the internal contention instigated by the king-men to overthrow the democratic judge system to establish a kingdom (see Alma 51 and Alma 61). During these times of internal contention and arguing, the Lamanites were able to conquer many cities that weren't sufficiently protected.

> *9 But behold, this was a critical time for such*
> *contentions to be among the people of Nephi;*
> *for behold, Amalickiah had again stirred*
> *up the hearts of the people of the Lamanites*
> *against the people of the Nephites, and he was*
> *gathering together soldiers from all parts of his*
> *land, and arming them, and preparing for war*
> *with all diligence; for he had sworn to drink*
> *the blood of Moroni.*
> *– Alma 51:9*

And, further witnessed in the following verses:

> *8 And now it came to pass that the armies of*
> *the Lamanites, on the west sea, south, while*

in the absence of Moroni on account of some intrigue amongst the Nephites, which caused dissensions amongst them, had gained some ground over the Nephites, yea, insomuch that they had obtained possession of a number of their cities in that part of the land.

9 And thus because of iniquity amongst themselves, yea, because of dissensions and intrigue among themselves they were placed in the most dangerous circumstances.
– Alma 53:8-9

The Nephites also lost ground because of those who chose to passively resist through their lack of commitment to the cause. Consider how this might happen when we choose to openly withdraw our support for another who needs our assistance with their battles:

13 And it came to pass that when the men who were called king-men had heard that the Lamanites were coming down to battle against them, they were glad in their hearts; and they refused to take up arms, for they were so wroth with the chief judge, and also with the people of liberty, that they would not take up arms to defend their country.

*14 And it came to pass that when Moroni saw
this, and also saw that the Lamanites were
coming into the borders of the land, he was
exceedingly wroth because of the stubbornness
of those people whom he had labored with
so much diligence to preserve; yea, he was
exceedingly wroth; his soul was filled with anger
against them.*
– Alma 51:13-14

Moroni summarizes well the effects of contention amongst ourselves and the division that results from pride and internal strife through the following verses:

*15 For were it not for the wickedness which
first commenced at our head, we could have
withstood our enemies that they could have
gained no power over us.*

*16 Yea, had it not been for the war which broke
out among ourselves; yea, were it not for these
king-men, who caused so much bloodshed
among ourselves; yea, at the time we were
contending among ourselves, if we had united
our strength as we hitherto have done; yea,
had it not been for the desire of power and
authority which those king-men had over us;
had they been true to the cause of our freedom,*

and united with us, and gone forth against
our enemies, instead of taking up their swords
against us, which was the cause of so much
bloodshed among ourselves; yea, if we had
gone forth against them in the strength of the
Lord, we should have dispersed our enemies,
for it would have been done, according to the
fulfilling of his word.

17 But behold, now the Lamanites are coming
upon us, taking possession of our lands, and
they are murdering our people with the sword,
yea, our women and our children, and also
carrying them away captive, causing them that
they should suffer all manner of afflictions, and
this because of the great wickedness of those
who are seeking for power and authority, yea,
even those king-men.
– Alma 60:15-17

When we examine history through the ages, we see a common theme between God's and Satan's efforts. All of God's work can be summarized into two words: **Connection** and **Unity**. All of Satan's work can likewise be summarized into two words: **Disconnection** and **Disunity**. We have discovered that contention, disconnection and disunity are at the root of every lost battle and every addiction. If we want to win, we must stop the in-fighting and see that we have only one enemy: Satan.

CHAPTER 8
Never a Happier Time

One of the most poignant messages taught by the war chapters in Alma is summarized by the following verses during a war between the Nephites and the Lamanites:

> *22 And those who were faithful in keeping the commandments of the Lord were delivered at all times, whilst thousands of their wicked brethren have been consigned to bondage, or to perish by the sword, or to dwindle in unbelief, and mingle with the Lamanites.*
>
> *23 But behold there never was a happier time among the people of Nephi, since the days of Nephi, than in the days of Moroni, yea, even at this time, in the twenty and first year of the reign of the judges.*
> *– Alma 50:22-23*

Though we fight a war everyday, if we will maintain our defenses and our protection against Satan, like the people of Nephi, we can live in a state of happiness amidst the war that is raging. In fact, these times can be the happiest of our lives.

Happiness is first a choice. The feeling of happiness follows the choice to **BE** happy regardless of the circumstances around us. We can choose to live our lives in anxious fear of constant attack or we can build our defenses strong and align ourselves with the Savior, knowing that he can protect us and deliver us from any attack.

From this position of strength, we can live in complete confidence and inner peace. The beauty of our alliance with Jesus Christ is that his Spirit always fills us with peace even when we need to stand our ground in the battle for liberty.

Is There Healing to Be Found From the Wounds of War?

Following the long wars, many were war-weary and wounded. However, we learn that there were two very different responses to the harrowing experiences that the Nephites faced in their fight for liberty.

> *41 But behold, because of the exceedingly great length of the war between the Nephites and the Lamanites many had become hardened, because of the exceedingly great length of the war; and many were softened because of their afflictions, insomuch that they did humble themselves before God, even in the depth of humility.*
> *– Alma 62:41*

Like the Nephites, we have the choice and the freedom to decide what meaning we will give to the experiences of our lives and the wars we have waged. We too can choose humility and allow these experiences to soften our hearts, or we can choose to harden our hearts and descend to a place of deeper darkness and disconnection.

Each experience is ours and the choice of how we react to that experience is ours. Our greatest liberty can come from knowing that we can choose to see every experience from an eye of humility. We can choose to allow every experience to draw us nearer to God and learn the lesson for which it was given.

CONCLUSION

How Will You Apply These Learnings?

The war chapters of Alma provide a wealth of lessons on maintaining and achieving greater self-mastery. They are not limited to the ones in this book. Many more await those willing to listen to the voice of revelation. The Book of Mormon was given to us by a loving God who inspired prophets to share these important lessons.

So, what is your next step? Hopefully you've gained some important insights in your battle for greater self-mastery. However, insight on its own will never produce transformation. Once we become aware of a new possibility for our lives, we don't 'know it;' we only 'know about it.' We are now "consciously incompetent" in new skills that we could master, or in other words we are now aware of skills that we do not yet possess or have not yet perfected.

So, how do you become "consciously competent" and deliberately develop these new skills? And ultimately, how do you achieve "unconscious competence" in self-mastery by performing habits without having to consciously think about them? This is a final lesson we can take from any great army, athlete, musician or expert in any field. We must **drill** what we desire to perfect relentlessly.

We encourage you to identify three areas of your life where you feel that you are 'holding your ground' in the area of self-mastery. Celebrate the success you have achieved. Ask yourself, "What can I do to fortify and strengthen those areas so that I can adequately maintain them against attack?"

Once you've done this, identify at least one to three areas of your life where you would like to achieve greater self-mastery. With the resources you have available, determine what you could begin today to gain further ground. Who could you enlist in your army of support to gain the additional strength needed to take that ground? Who are the experts that are a few rungs further up the ladder of awareness who could help? And, what could you apply from the principles shared here to take further ground in your quest for greater self-mastery?

Put your plan in place. Write it down. Determine your purpose, and enlist yourself fully in the battle. Surround yourself with the support you need.

Most importantly, strengthen your alliance with the One who has already conquered all foes and will certainly help you conquer yours. You can choose to start winning today as you fight with and for your Savior, Jesus Christ who will help you achieve success in any battle.

Awaken Your Warrior

As you enlist yourself in the battle and align with the Savior, consider Captain Moroni's rallying call to the entire Nephite Nation:

> *Behold whosever will maintain this title upon the land, let them come forth in the strength of the Lord, and enter into a covenant that they will maintain their rights, and their religion, that the Lord God will bless them.*
> *– Alma 46:20*

We live in a time of Psychological and Spiritual warfare; a time when Marriages and Families are being subtly devastated by distortions of love and the trauma of betrayal.

As in the days of the Book of Mormon, to win these battles we must not remain isolated; we must gather as Divine Warriors. Mothers must gather as "Mothers Who Know" for support against Satan's lies and shame-filled attacks. Fathers must gather as the Men of Moroni who are trained to discern the infiltrations of spiritual warfare and respond with the same protective ferocity that Jesus used when cleansing the temple. And, youth must gather as the Sons of Helaman, training with exactness to win the war of self-mastery that no one believes they can win.

We invite you to **not** fight this war as the Enemy would have you fight: **Isolated** and **Unskilled**. We invite you, before the pain and injuries have started, before tears turn into devastation, to begin fighting for your Freedom and your Families....

For men who have experienced significant attacks on their sexual self mastery, including impulsive pornography use beyond their values system, look into the Men of Moroni training system. *(Visit **LifeChangingServices.org** for more information on the program.)*

For your young men who need advanced sexual self-mastery training, consider the Sons of Helaman training program. *(Visit **LifeChangingServices.org** for more information on the program.)*

For daughters and adult women who need clinical self-mastery training of all forms, look into the Daughters of Light. *(Visit **LifeChangingServices.org** for more information on the program.)*

For all family members desiring to train themselves in powerful tactics that protect against enemy attacks before they lead to addictive behaviors and to significant lost battles, consider the Eternal Warriors Program. *(Visit **EternalWarriorsTraining. org** for more information on the program.)*

For mothers who need support and guidance on how to help a family member who is struggling, consider the Mothers Who Know program. *(Visit **MothersWhoKnow.org** for more information on the program.)*

And finally, if you are a wife who has unfortunately been traumatized by your husband's lack of sexual self-mastery, consider the WORTH group. *(Visit **LifeChangingServices.org/ Worth** for more information on the program.)*

It is our greatest desire to serve you well as you Awaken Your Warrior and step fully into the fight for all that you love and hold dear.

To learn more about Life Changing Services and all of its programs for addiction prevention, recovery and self-mastery, visit our websites at:

www.LifeChangingServices.org

and

www.EternalWarriorsTraining.org

Hello, this is Maurice Harker, the author of *Like Dragons Did They Fight*, a companion to *Never A Happier Time*.

I want you to have a free copy of *Like Dragons Did They Fight*.

I worked for 10 years before becoming a mental health counselor to discover and clarify the principles you will read in this book. My question was, "Why do good, smart people do things that contradict their values system?"

Since I became a mental health counselor 15 years ago, I have refined my understanding of the principles while working with real people in real-life situations and have refined the writing of those principles.

I am honored and reverenced that, as of 2020, over 50,000 people have received copies of this book, both in eBook form as well as in paperback and I want you to have it as well; for yourself, for your youth, for our spouse, and for those within your stewardship.

I hope it helps. I have dedicated my life to providing you and your loved one with Life Changing Services.

Go to LikeDragonsFree.com to receive a copy now.